Development and Pilot Test of the **RAND Program Evaluation Toolkit** for COUNTERING VIOLENT EXTREMISM

Sina Beaghley, Todd C. Helmus,
Miriam Matthews, Rajeev Ramchand,
David Stebbins, Amanda Kadlec, Michael A. Brown

Prepared for the Department of Homeland Security
Approved for public release; distribution unlimited

For more information on this publication, visit www.rand.org/t/RR1799

Library of Congress Cataloging-in-Publication Data is available for this publication.
ISBN: 978-0-8330-9725-5

Published by the RAND Corporation, Santa Monica, Calif.
© Copyright 2017 RAND Corporation
RAND® is a registered trademark.

*Cover images: Albany Associates/Flickr (top); hxdbzxy/GettyImages (middle);
teekid/GettyImages (bottom).*

Support RAND
Make a tax-deductible charitable contribution at
www.rand.org/giving/contribute

www.rand.org

Preface

The White House's 2016 *Strategic Implementation Plan for Empowering Local Partners to Prevent Violent Extremism in the United States* recommends "proactive actions to counter efforts by extremists to recruit, radicalize, and mobilize followers to violence." Such actions should seek to address the conditions and reduce the underlying factors that give rise to radicalization and recruitment (Executive Office of the President, 2016, p. 2). Evaluations are critical to assessing the impact of programs focused on countering violent extremism (CVE) and can inform decisions about whether to sustain, scale up, or discontinue program activities. The U.S. Department of Homeland Security's Office of Community Partnerships asked the RAND Corporation to create a toolkit to guide future evaluations of community-initiated CVE activities and programs.

The overall goal of the toolkit is to help those responsible for CVE programs determine whether their activities produce beneficial effects, to identify areas for improvement, and, ultimately, to guide the responsible allocation of scarce resources.

The toolkit is based on RAND's Getting To Outcomes® approach, an evidenced-based model designed to help community-based programs conduct self-evaluations. It was specifically adapted from the RAND Suicide Prevention Program Evaluation Toolkit (Acosta et al., 2013), with adaptations informed by a review of the peer-reviewed literature, interviews with staff from U.S.-based CVE programs, and feedback from staff responsible for implementing CVE programs, collected as part of a pilot test of the toolkit.

This companion report summarizes the methods used to develop the RAND Program Evaluation Toolkit for Countering Violent Extremism and provides additional background on the toolkit's development. The toolkit is available at www.rand.org/t/TL243.

This report will be of particular interest to managers and directors of community-based CVE programs, as well as program funders. Although the toolkit is tailored to the needs of evaluators with limited prior experience, this account of its development may also be of interest to academic program evaluation experts who assist programs with evaluations or conduct studies of program effectiveness.

This research was sponsored by the Office of Community Partnerships in the U.S. Department of Homeland Security and conducted in the International Security and Defense Policy Center of the RAND National Defense Research Institute, a federally funded research and development center sponsored by the Office of the Secretary of Defense, the Joint Staff, the Unified Combatant Commands, the Navy, the Marine Corps, the defense agencies, and the defense Intelligence Community.

For more information on the RAND International Security and Defense Policy Center, see www.rand.org/nsrd/ndri/centers/isdp or contact the director (contact information is provided on the web page).

Contents

Figure and Tables

Figure

Tables

Summary

Evaluations of programs and activities can provide valuable information to guide program development, implementation, and modification. Such evaluations are critical for programs that seek to counter violent extremism (CVE), such as efforts by extremists to recruit, radicalize, and mobilize followers to violence. The RAND Program Evaluation Toolkit for Countering Violent Extremism is designed to support program self-evaluation and help those responsible for CVE programs determine whether their activities produce beneficial effects and outcomes.

This companion report summarizes the methods used to develop the toolkit (Helmus et al., 2017) and provides additional background on its development.

Development of the CVE Program Evaluation Toolkit

We used three complementary methods to develop the toolkit: a systematic review of the CVE program evaluation literature; interviews with 30 managers of U.S.-based CVE programs, during which we asked about the programs' activities and challenges of CVE program assessment; and a pilot test of the toolkit in collaboration with representatives from three CVE programs.

Literature Review

We conducted a systematic review of the CVE program evaluation literature to identify the types of evaluation approaches and measures used elsewhere. We were able to find only eight sources that assessed the impact of CVE programming.[1] They covered a wide array of CVE interventions, from the U.S. Agency for International Development's CVE programming in Africa to studies that sought to help Muslim populations that had recently migrated to Europe better manage issues of identity and multiculturalism. There was also an innovative study designed to test a program in which former extremists sought to conduct deradicalization engagements with extremists on Facebook (Frenett and Dow, 2014). Overall, these findings suggest that CVE initiatives hold promise and are worthy of further scientific study. However, we highlight two key limitations in this body of work. First, the number of available research studies is too small to inform the development or funding of new CVE programs. Only four of the eight studies examined CVE programs in Western countries; this posed a challenge because we set out to design a toolkit primarily for U.S.-based programs. Second, only a lim-

---

[1] These sources are listed in the references section of this report: Aldrich (2014); Frenett and Dow (2014); Feddes, Mann, and Doosje (2015); Amjad and Wood (2009); Liht and Savage (2013); Williams, Horgan, and Evans (2011); and U.S. Agency for International Development (2011, 2013).

ited number of studies utilized control groups. We believe it will be critical to produce more rigorous investigations that randomly assign participants to treatment and control groups or at least incorporate pre/post investigations with a control group.

Interviews with U.S.-Based CVE Program Managers and Profiles of CVE Program Activities

To tailor the toolkit to specific needs of U.S.-based CVE programs, we conducted an online search that identified 95 such programs that focused on Islamist or right-wing extremism. We interviewed 30 CVE program managers, discussing specific program interventions, goals, and existent approaches to program evaluation. We used input from these interviews to categorize and code each program's target population, intervention objectives, activity types, and output and outcomes. This information guided the development of the toolkit logic model and a menu of potential metrics for program evaluation.

We also analyzed the data we had collected during our interviews to identify challenges that CVE programs may face as they seek to assess their outcomes. We learned that few programs collected information on long-term outcomes. Although several program managers indicated that they collected data on short-term outcomes or program outputs, almost none provided details on any analyses of these data. When discussing barriers to the collection of metrics and conducting program evaluations more broadly, interviewees often described resource limitations and confusion, or a lack of knowledge, regarding program evaluation.

Pilot Testing the Toolkit

We sought feedback on a preliminary draft of our toolkit from three organizations that participated in our interviews: One program focused on curbing Islamist extremism, and two addressed extremism more broadly. Chapter Three describes the process used to engage these program staff and elicit their feedback on the toolkit. It also summarizes the feedback we received and revisions made to the toolkit as a result of this feedback.

The program staff who agreed to participate in the pilot test were asked to read through the toolkit over a two-week period and complete the toolkit's worksheets, checklists, and templates. They were then asked to provide feedback using a standardized form, which they returned via email upon completion.

Conclusions

The goal of the RAND Program Evaluation Toolkit for Countering Violent Extremism is to build the knowledge and skills of those responsible for implementing CVE programs in support of program self-evaluation. Such evaluations are critical to assessing the program impact and can inform decisions about whether to, sustain, scale up, or discontinue program activities. We developed the toolkit with the hope that it would serve as a helpful resource to guide CVE programs in assessing their activities, identifying areas for improvement, measuring the outcomes, and making adjustments to their programs—all of which can ultimately reduce the risk of violent extremism in their communities.

Acknowledgments

We gratefully acknowledge the work and assistance of the 30 community-based CVE programs that agreed to participate in interviews to inform the development of our evaluation toolkit. We are also grateful to the three anonymous CVE program managers who reviewed drafts of our assessment toolkit and provided recommendations for improvement. Special thanks also goes to the U.S. Department of Homeland Security's Office of Community Partnerships, which funded this study. We are also indebted to Jennifer Bryson of the Center for Islam and Religious Freedom and Scott Savitz at RAND, who provided considered critiques of this report and the companion toolkit. Any errors are the sole responsibility of the study's authors.

CHAPTER ONE

Introduction and Overview

Violent extremism poses a serious threat to the lives of those living in the United States and abroad. The nature of extremist violence varies, as do its motivations. Those who perpetuate these acts may be motivated by an ideology (e.g., extremist religious beliefs), a specific issue (e.g., animal liberation), or a separatist/political cause. For example, the Islamic State has recruited more than 27,000 foreign fighters, 6,000 of whom are Westerners (Kirk, 2016). Other forms of extremism (e.g., right- and left-wing extremism) also pose significant threats: Since September 11, 2001, domestic terrorists have killed 48 people in the United States, and 182 domestic extremists have been indicted, convicted, or killed (New America Foundation, 2015). *Domestic terrorists* are those who "commit crimes within the homeland and draw inspiration from U.S.-based extremist ideologies and movements" (Bjelopera, 2013, p. 6).[1] These ideologies include extremist views associated with neo-Nazism, white supremacy, black separatism, neofascism, and anti-government or anti-abortion movements, as well as animal rights and environmental protection.

There are many community-led programs that focus on countering violent extremism in the United States and Canada. These programs represent a critical tool in the fight against all forms of extremism. However, little is known about their effectiveness. This limits the degree to which private donor organizations or governments can make informed decisions about program improvements and whether to sustain, scale up, or discontinue program activities.

Need for a CVE Program Evaluation Toolkit

Efforts that help promote scientific assessments of CVE programming are critical. Evaluations can assess the impact of program activities to counter violent extremism (CVE) and can inform decisions about whether to sustain, scale up, or discontinue current efforts. The overall goal of the RAND Program Evaluation Toolkit for Countering Violent Extremism is to help those responsible for CVE programs determine whether their activities produce beneficial effects, to identify areas for improvement, and, ultimately, to guide the responsible allocation of scarce resources. This toolkit was adapted from the RAND Suicide Prevention Program Evaluation Toolkit (Acosta et al., 2013).

---

[1] This definition differs slightly from that in U.S. Code, Title 18, Section 2331, which defines *domestic terrorism* as terrorist attacks that "occur primarily within the territorial jurisdiction of the United States." This definition is neutral regarding the type of terrorist actor.

Purpose of This Report

This companion report summarizes the methods used to adapt and develop the toolkit. The toolkit has three specific aims:

1. to help CVE program managers design an evaluation according to their program type and available resources and expertise
2. to support the selection of measures for new evaluations and augment or enhance ongoing evaluations
3. to offer basic guidance on how to analyze evaluation data and then use these data to improve the effectiveness of CVE programs.

We used a multistep process to ensure that the toolkit accomplished these aims and was appropriately adapted for community-based CVE programs. First, we conducted a systematic review of the CVE program evaluation literature to identify the types of evaluation approaches and measures used elsewhere. Then, we interviewed CVE program managers, mostly representing U.S.-based programs, about their activities and their assessment processes. Our initial search identified almost 100 CVE programs and activities, and we conducted interviews with 30 program managers. These helped us tailor the toolkit's logic model to the unique needs of U.S.-based CVE programs. We also analyzed information collected during these interviews on challenges to CVE program assessment. Finally, we pilot tested the toolkit and elicited feedback from a subgroup of CVE program managers. We then revised the toolkit based on this feedback.

Organization of This Report

The remainder of this report is organized as follows. Chapter Two provides detail about how the initial draft of the toolkit was developed. Chapter Three summarizes the toolkit's pilot test, including how we elicited feedback on the initial draft and revisions that we made in response to this feedback. Chapter Four presents conclusions regarding toolkit implementation and intended uses.

CHAPTER TWO

Development of the CVE Program Evaluation Toolkit

The process that we used to develop the toolkit consisted of three steps. First, we conducted a literature review of prior studies of CVE programs, including evaluation studies of such programs. Next, we identified almost 100 organizations based mostly in the United States that had a CVE component as part of a broader program objective or as their core function. We interviewed program managers from 30 of those organizations about their activities and their assessment processes. Finally, we analyzed the interview data to identify challenges that CVE programs may face as they seek to assess their outcomes. All of these steps served to inform the development of the toolkit.

Literature Review

Our literature review focused on relevant academic, military, and other publicly available sources describing how CVE programs in the United States and elsewhere are assessed, monitored, and evaluated.

Methods

We conducted our document search in two phases. First, we searched academic databases on the phrase *countering violent extremism* in tandem with the following terms and variants of the following terms: *assessment, monitoring, evaluation, metrics, prevention, messaging, community, at risk, counternarrative, deradicalization, postradicalization,* or *counter-radicalization.*[1] This approach initially yielded more than 200 results. We searched additional promising bibliographies to ensure that our literature search did not miss any key documents.[2] We specifically searched for reports that sought to link a CVE intervention to measurable outcomes. We defined CVE *interventions* as those that aim to (1) prevent populations from adopting violent extremist ideologies (primary prevention), (2) halt and reverse the spread of those ideologies among populations that show indications or warning signs (secondary prevention), and (3) "deradicalize" populations that have already engaged in violent extremist activities (tertiary prevention; see Williams, Horgan, and Evans, 2016). Ultimately, of the hundreds of articles

---

[1] We used these search terms to locate resources in the following academic databases: JSTOR, PubMed, Thompson Reuters, ProQuest Military, EBSCO, SAGE, and Lexis-Nexis.

[2] Examples include Feddes and Gallucci (2015–2016) and Romaniuk (2015)

reviewed as part of this process, we were able to identify only eight sources that linked a CVE intervention to outcomes (see Table 2.1).[3]

Results and Common Themes

Appendix A of this report summarizes the methodology and findings of these eight studies, along with overarching observations.

It was noteworthy that only four studies examined the impact of CVE programming in either the United States or Europe. One study was based in Pakistan (Amjad and Wood, 2009), and three studies examined the impact of USAID programming in Africa (Aldrich, 2014; USAID, 2011, 2013).[4] Of the remaining CVE investigations, one was based in the Netherlands (Feddes, Mann, and Doosje, 2015) and one in the United Kingdom (Liht and Savage, 2013). These latter two efforts sought to help Muslim populations that had recently migrated to Europe better manage issues of identity and multiculturalism. In another study, investigators used Facebook analytics to identify samples of individuals in North America and

Table 2.1
Research Studies That Linked CVE Interventions to Outcomes

Location	Source
Africa	Daniel P. Aldrich, "First Steps Towards Hearts and Minds? USAID's Countering Violent Extremism Policies in Africa," *Terrorism and Political Violence*, Vol. 26, No. 3, 2014, pp. 523–546
	U.S. Agency for International Development (USAID), *Mid-Term Evaluation of USAID's Counter-Extremism Programming in Africa*, Washington, D.C., February 1, 2011
	USAID, *Mid-Term Evaluation of Three Countering Violent Extremism Projects, Counter-Extremism Programming in Africa*, Washington, D.C., February 22, 2013
Pakistan	Naumana Amjad and Alex M. Wood, "Identifying and Changing the Normative Beliefs About Aggression Which Lead Young Muslim Adults to Join Extremist Anti-Semitic Groups in Pakistan," *Aggressive Behavior*, Vol. 35, No. 6, November–December 2009, pp. 514–519
Europe	Jose Liht and Sara Savage, "Preventing Violent Extremism Through Value Complexity: Being Muslim Being British," *Journal of Strategic Security*, Vol. 6, No. 4, Winter 2013, pp. 44–66
	Allard R. Feddes, Liesbeth Mann, and Bertjan Doosje, "Increasing Self-Esteem and Empathy to Prevent Violent Radicalization: A Longitudinal Quantitative Evaluation of a Resilience Training Focused on Adolescents with a Dual Identity," *Journal of Applied Social Psychology*, Vol. 45, No. 7, July 2015, pp. 400–411
Europe/United States	Frenett, Ross, and Moli Dow, *One to One Interventions: A Pilot CVE Methodology*, London: Institute for Strategic Dialogue, Curtain University, 2014
United States	Michael Williams, John G. Horgan, and William P. Evans, *Evaluation of a Multi-Faceted, U.S. Community-Based, Muslim-Led CVE Program*, report submitted to the U.S. Department of Justice, June 2016

---

[3] After our literature review was complete, we identified two evaluations of counternarrative campaigns (one of which was published after our review) that reviewed engagement on social media and included qualitative reviews of users' comments (Reynolds and Tuck, 2016; Al-Rawi, 2013), as well as an Australian survey of adolescents that inquired about perspectives on past campaigns (Richardson, 2013).

[4] While USAID should be lauded for its evaluation efforts, the type of programming described in these studies likely has little relevance to Western community-based CVE efforts.

the United Kingdom who appeared to actively support far-right or Islamist extremist groups. They then recruited former extremists to directly engage with these users through Facebook's Messenger application (Frenett and Dow, 2015). Only one study was devoted to assessing a U.S. community-based CVE program. As part of a National Institute of Justice–sponsored initiative, those researchers examined the impact of a tripartite program from the World Organization for Resource Development and Education (WORDE) that included community education, volunteer and multicultural programs, and collaboration between law enforcement and community partners (Williams, Horgan, and Evans, 2016).

Overall, the methodological approaches of these studies varied considerably. Only one study used the most rigorous methodological approach: the random assignment of participants to either a treatment or control condition (Amjad and Wood, 2009). In this study, researchers randomly assigned students at the University of Pakistan to attend a lecture designed to help participants develop empathy toward Jews (the treatment condition) or a lecture on cognitive behavioral therapy (control condition).[5]

Other studies used various alternatives to test program impact. Two used a pre/post design (Feddes, Mann, and Doosje, 2015; Liht and Savage, 2013). In a Dutch study of 46 youth with migrant backgrounds, researchers assessed program outcomes by administering questionnaires to participants at baseline, during treatment, and after treatment and examined the level of improvement over time (Feddes, Mann, and Doosje, 2015).[6] Liht and Savage (2013) used a slightly different metric: comparing coding of qualitative content from small-group discussions held both prior to and after the initiation of treatment. USAID evaluations surveyed residents in cities that were exposed or not exposed USAID programming and compared differences in outcomes (Aldrich, 2014; USAID 2011, 2013).

Finally, other studies used no control group at all. In the study that examined the impact of Facebook messaging (Frenett and Dow, 2015), investigators did not use a control group to assess impact per se, but instead examined extremist responses as a function of the different communication styles employed by the former extremists. Williams, Horgan, and Evans (2016) also did not use a control group. Instead, they examined participant responses on a seven-point Likert scale weighted from completely disagree (1) to neither agree nor disagree (4) to completely agree (7) and looked for mean item responses that exceeded the threshold for "neither agree nor disagree."

Virtually all of these studies, to one degree or another, reported positive outcomes. The USAID programs were able to demonstrate success in some but not all anticipated outcomes. Aldrich (2014), for example, found that program participants in Timbuktu, Mali, were more likely than nonparticipants in a neighboring area to report listening to peaceful radio programs and participating in community decisionmaking.[7] However, the program was not able to improve perceptions about whether the United States was fighting Islam or the justifications for al-Qa'ida's activities. In the Dutch intervention, post-treatment questionnaires showed that three workshops designed to help migrant Muslims manage issues of identity and multi-

---

[5] This particular treatment was developed based on the results of an earlier study showing that normative beliefs about aggression against Jews were strong predictors of whether an individual agreed to join an anti-Semitic extremist organization.

[6] These questionnaires measured variables that were theorized to be affected by training: agency, attitudes toward violence, violent intentions, self-esteem, and perspective taking, or the act of viewing an issue or situation from an alternative perspective.

[7] The outcome "listening to peaceful radio programs" is more likely a measure of performance rather than impact.

culturalism led to self-reported improvements in agency and attitudes toward ideology-based violence and participants' own violent intentions. Other key outcomes reached only trend levels of statistical significance, however (Feddes, Mann, and Doosje, 2015).[8] Most recently, participants in WORDE's CVE program reported improvements on 12 of 14 surveyed items (Williams, Horgan, and Evans, 2016).[9] And Frenett and Dow (2015) showed that 59 percent of extremists on Facebook responded to anti-radicalization messages by either replying directly to the original message or by blocking the service. Of the responders, 60 percent entered into a sustained engagement with the former radicals. The researchers also showed that a casual, sentimental, or reflective tone on the part of the former radicals elicited the most engagement from the extremists.

Overall, these findings suggest that CVE initiatives hold promise and are worthy of further scientific study. There are at least two key limitations with this body of work. First, the number of available research studies is too small to effectively inform the development of new CVE programming, guide program improvements, or help policymakers and donors decide whether to sustain, scale up, or discontinue program activities. Because our toolkit is intended primarily for U.S.-based CVE programs, this shortfall was particularly striking in that only four studies were conducted in Western countries. Second, while we laud the effort put forth by the researchers whose studies we reviewed, it will be critical to produce more rigorous investigations that randomly assign participants to treatment and control groups or at least feature pre/post investigations with a control group. Otherwise, it will be difficult to assert a strong confidence in these research findings.

Interviews with U.S.-Based CVE Program Managers and Profiles of CVE Program Activities

A key element of the toolkit is its logic model. A logic model is a graphical depiction of the key elements of a program that includes available resources, target audience, program activities and corresponding objectives, intended outcomes, and community needs being filled. Completing a logic model helps program evaluators tie specific program activities to specific intermediate outcomes and, ultimately, to appropriate evaluation methods and tools. The most challenging aspect of creating the logic model in the toolkit was ensuring that we included an appropriate menu of CVE-relevant options for program activities and objectives. To gauge the needs of CVE programs, we conducted a series of interviews with representatives from 30 programs.

We conducted a web-based search and identified 95 programs focused on countering Islamist (45.3 percent; n = 43 programs) and other forms of extremism (54.7 percent; n = 52). Overall, 10.5 percent (n = 10) of programs either did not qualify or were no longer active, leaving a total of 85 programs. Of this total, we interviewed representatives from 30 programs (35.3 percent). Of the remaining 55 programs, 63.6 percent (n = 35) did not respond, 16.4 percent (n = 9) refused to participate, and 10.9 percent (n = 6) had no publicly available contact

---

[8] *Trend levels of statistical significance* refers to findings that have a p-value that is close to but ultimately not below 0.05. The study found only marginal improvements in self-esteem, empathy, and perspective taking.

[9] Each of these items consisted of single questions addressing different types of outcomes. For example, "I feel welcome," "I have responsibilities," and "I feel accepted."

information.[10] We conducted interviews with representatives of the 30 participating programs between January and June 2016. These interviews were structured to elicit information about specific program intervention activities, goals, and approaches to program evaluation.

Our analysis focused on the subset of 25 organizations that were based in the United States, that sought to use their programming to counter violent extremism, and that were not, themselves, advocacy or research organizations. Some programs had a CVE component as part of a broader program objective; for others, CVE-based activities were the program's core function. Based on the interviews, we identified 46 distinct activities or interventions initiated by these organizations.[11] We then used the descriptions of these activities and interventions to categorize and code them by activity type, target population, intervention objective, and any outputs or outcomes they produced or were intended to produce. Ultimately, we applied this information to the development of the toolkit's logic model and to craft a menu of potential metrics for CVE program evaluation.

Categorization and Coding

Of the 46 activities that we coded, 63 percent (n = 29) were focused on countering Islamist extremism, and the remaining 37 percent (n = 17) focused on other forms of extremism. We then categorized each activity's target population, intervention goal, activity type, and outputs and outcomes. We caution that there were several limitations in the application of codes to program operations. First, the programs we examined may not be representative of all CVE programs based in the United States. We recognize, for example, that our initial web search to capture U.S.-based CVE programs likely missed a number of relevant programs. Second, our coding of programs' target populations, intervention goals, activity types, and program outputs and outcomes was inherently subjective, informed by interviews with CVE program managers. The process involved some imputation on the part of the coders in classifying program operations. Ultimately, the purpose was less to scientifically quantify program characteristics than to gain a general understanding of the CVE landscape to inform the toolkit's development and to, in turn, help CVE program managers classify and evaluate their own programs. These managers may well classify their target audiences, activities, and objectives differently.

Target Audience

Based on an initial review of the program data, we developed a two-part taxonomy for classifying a CVE program's target audience. We coded each activity as attempting to influence either an *individual* who is at risk of becoming a violent extremist or a community or community members who can, in turn, influence individuals who are at risk. A program may also seek to target both populations. Of the 46 activities that we identified, 12 (26 percent) targeted at-risk individuals, 20 (43 percent) targeted other community members, and 14 (30 percent) possessed characteristics of both in roughly equal parts.

For example, one Washington, D.C.–based organization sought to help youth aged 13–18 develop the skills to effectively distinguish true Islamic principles from extremist ideology. It also provided these youth with a safe space to ask questions about extremism. This activity focuses on at-risk individuals. However, another activity run by the same organization was considered community-focused. In this activity, the organization sought to directly engage

---

[10] The 35.3-percent response rate for these interviews falls within the typical response rate range for these types of studies.

[11] Organizations frequently engage in more than one type of activity or intervention.

parents and community leaders to help increase community members' understanding of the threat of terrorism and what they should do if they see a threat. Finally, program activities can focus on both at-risk individuals and community members who can influence individuals who are at risk. For example, a New Jersey organization worked to counter racism by holding workshops to not only help participants identify and correct their own internalized racism but also to show how they could work within the community to address societal racism.

Intervention Objectives

We used grounded theory analysis (Glaser and Strauss, 1967) to categorize and code activity objectives. We listed each activity objective or set of objectives and combined similar objectives into a singular category if they were mentioned several times. The team then discussed the objectives as a group and decided on a common category objective. Using this approach, program objectives were best categorized separately between those activities that target individuals at risk of extremism and their surrounding communities.

Objectives for individual-focused programs or activities were as follows:

- Counter violent extremist/racist opinions and ideology.
- Improve psychological conditions/address moral concerns.
- Enhance positive social networks.
- Reduce political grievances.
- Improve social/economic integration.

Objectives for community-focused programs or activities were as follows:

- Help community members understand and identify violent extremism and risks.
- Build capacity of community members to identify/engage with at-risk individuals.
- Build capacity of positive and influential community members or leaders to credibly counter violent extremist ideology.
- Create environments accepting of minority groups.
- Promote policies that address political grievances.
- Strengthen government capacity to curtail violent extremism.

Of a total of 26 activities with a focus on influencing at-risk individuals, the overwhelming majority (n = 24) sought to counter violent extremist opinions and ideology, and just over a third (n = 9) aimed to enhance social networks. Roughly a tenth focused on improving psychological conditions (n = 4), reducing political or social grievances (n = 3), or economic integration (n = 3).

Of a total of 34 activities that sought to influence a community or community members who can, in turn, influence individuals who are at risk, the most common objective was helping communities understand violent extremism and racism (n = 31) and building the capacity of positive and influential community members to more actively counter extremism (n = 24). Another 13 activities sought to help communities identify or engage with at-risk individuals. Approximately 20 percent of activities sought to promote policies that addressed grievances associated with extremism (n = 8) or help strengthen government capacity to curtail violent extremism/racism (n = 6). Three sought to counter Islamophobia in the broader community and to create environments that were accepting of minority groups.

Activity Type

Using the same approach for cataloguing objectives (i.e., grounded theory analysis), we categorized program activities into one of the following: (1) communication, (2) training/education, (3) counseling, or (4) group/social activities.

Of the organizations interviewed, most (n = 28) pursued activities under the training/education rubric. Specific activities ranged from individual or group workshops to targeted education trainings for government administrators. Also commonly reported were communication activities, such as online campaigns or film productions and screenings disseminated to a targeted or broad public audience. Organizations reported 12 group/social activities, including Boy Scouts and after-school programs. Counseling efforts accounted for only two reported activities.

Program/Activity Output and Outcomes

Program outputs are the amount, quality, or volume of goods or services provided by a program; *program outcomes* are changes in the target population expected as a result of engaging in the program activities. Overall, few programs collected systematic data on outcomes: None collected long-term outcome data, and few collected short-term outcome data. This aligns with the observations in previous research of CVE program evaluation (see, e.g., Mastroe and Szmania, 2016). However, many more programs collected output data on their activities. Figure 2.1 shows examples of the type of output data that can be collected according to particular activity types.

We asked interviewees to provide information about what, if any, data they collected on their program, including data on their program's effectiveness. If they collected program data, we asked how administrators had used these data to inform changes to the program. If they did not collect program data, we asked interviewees to indicate why they did not collect data. In addition, we asked all interviewees questions about challenges to assessment. We coded interview notes addressing these questions for content and then analyzed them to identify key themes.

Figure 2.1
Activity Types and Outputs

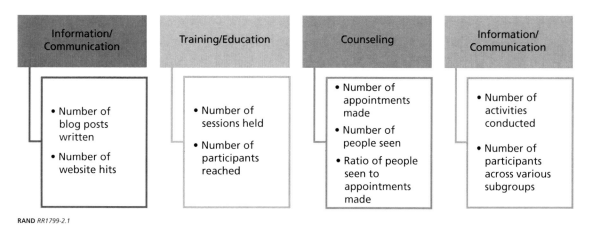

RAND RR1799-2.1

Output Metrics

Administrators from eight of the programs indicated that they collected data on program outputs, which involved assessments of activities performed or who participated in the programs. Output metrics included media mentions of the program, the number of registered website users, the number of users on the program's mailing list, the number of individuals exposed to the program (e.g., the number who saw a film), and email feedback regarding program components. Interviewees provided little or no information about how output data were used to improve program performance or reach.

Short-Term Outcomes

Administrators from eight of the programs indicated that they collected data on short-term outcomes, or immediate program impacts. All of of our interviewees noted that they administered surveys immediately following program participation. Information collected through these surveys included participants' perceptions of changes in knowledge and attitudes about the issue of concern, knowledge regarding the issue of concern, engagement in activities to address the issue, and perceptions of the program's efficacy in addressing the issue. One program, which helped train youth to create and implement their own CVE programs, included assessments that were conducted immediately before and after activities to gauge changes in participants' knowledge and attitudes. Another program that ran a series of activities for youth at a mosque, including summer camps and youth dialogue sessions, also sought to collect feedback from participants. According to the administrator, in addition to collecting post-activity surveys, "we interview young people, talk to parents, and see how the kids participate in activities of the mosque."

Interviewees provided limited information about analyses of the data collected. One interviewee mentioned collecting data on the proportion of participants who perceived that the program had changed their attitudes. Others cited survey participants' positive comments regarding the programs. Another, the administrator of the mosque youth program, described measuring how many kids came back to the activities and how they get involved. That program also used these metrics to make adjustments to programming. The administrator noted, "If [we learn that the program is] too lecture-heavy, then [we] change to more activities."

Long-Term Outcomes

Only two interviewees mentioned any effort to assess long-term outcomes. One interviewee, who was involved with a program that organized an anti-racism summer institute, reported that program administrators collected information on long-term program outcomes. Specifically, administrators collected data from individuals before their participation and again several times after participation, including a few months, one year, three years, and five years later. However, administrators had not had the time or resources to conduct a close analysis of these data. Another program collected assorted success stories from an initiative designed to help youth become more active in advocating for peace and reconciliation. Staff were able to document several instances in which youth were able to take the lessons they had learned in their training and develop new and independent peace-building initiatives.

Another interviewee ran a program that included mass-media messaging and used social media metrics to track media hits and repetition of program narratives. This administrator added that the program tracked changes in targeted public policies and decreases in fundraising for extremist groups. However, the administrator shared limited information about when and how the data were collected, how they were analyzed, and what the results revealed.

Challenges to CVE Program Evaluation

Previous research suggests that few CVE programs participate in or perform evaluations of their activities (Mastroe and Szmania, 2016). Of the CVE programs in our study that did collect data, they generally collected descriptive program information with little or no consideration of data or documentation on program efficacy, also known as program outcomes. This lack of suitable data inhibits conclusions about which CVE programs, or which elements of CVE programs, are effective, which programs and elements may benefit from modifications, and which should be discontinued.

Researchers have suggested several factors that may contribute to a lack of CVE program evaluation. These factors include different definitions of extremism across CVE programs, difficulty assessing whether a program has effectively deterred individuals from engaging in extremist acts (e.g., assessing a program's contribution to the absence of a behavior), and limited resources for data collection and analysis (Fink, Romaniuk, and Barakat, 2013; Romaniuk, 2015). To better understand the assessment efforts of and challenges faced by CVE program administrators, we asked interviewees several questions about evaluation.

Interviewees gave several reasons for the limited or nonexistent collection of data by CVE programs. However, most comments highlighted two factors: resource limitations and confusion regarding evaluation.

Resource Limitations

Several interviewees suggested that they did not have the resources available to conduct systematic program evaluations. For example, one interviewee stated, "Assessments? No, not really. I worked with evaluation and assessments in my whole career, but I can't keep up with it. We don't have the staff to track things." Similarly, another interviewee's program did not have the ability to track participants over multiple years, preventing administrators from assessing long-term program outcomes.

Given their limited program resources, interviewees commented that they preferred to devote all available resources to program implementation. Thus, program evaluation was not an immediate concern. According to one interviewee, "We do need some data to indicate [in] what places we are strong and where we could be more effective. But when you have momentum, you don't work on that." Another commented, "Why waste time on metrics when [we] don't have time? [It's a] distant priority."

Confusion About Evaluation

Interviewees also noted that few, if any, staff were familiar with program evaluation, and they were uncertain how to design, administer, or analyze the results of a program evaluation. For example, interviewees did not know how to analyze longitudinal data or what measures to collect as part of a program evaluation. One interviewee thought that many available data-collection options, such as Likert scales, did not provide useful information for the program. Several interviewees were also uncertain about how to measure and demonstrate a counterfactual, such as the absence of extremist behaviors.

Finally, interviewees expressed concern about whether being asked to complete a survey could affect participants' perceptions of the program. For example, they worried that participants would view a survey as intrusive and may have limited familiarity with or interest in supporting program evaluation. According to one interviewee, "Anything with government funding is not trusted. A lot of results you can perceive anecdotally, [but] to track what is working and not working is a fool's errand."

Summary of Challenges

In interviews with CVE program administrators, we asked questions about their collection of various metrics and limitations to the collection of metrics. Few collected information about the long-term outcomes of their programs. Although several indicated that they collected data on short-term outcomes or program outputs, almost none of those interviewed described the results of these collection efforts. When discussing barriers to the collection of metrics and CVE program evaluation more broadly, interviewees often mentioned resource limitations, confusion about evaluation procedures, and a lack of knowledge about program evaluation.

Pilot Testing the Toolkit

We sought feedback on a preliminary draft of our toolkit from three organizations that participated in our interviews: One program focused on curbing Islamist extremism, and two address extremism more broadly. This chapter describes the process used to engage these program staff and elicit their feedback. It also summarizes the feedback we received and revisions made to the toolkit as a result of this feedback.

We asked the three program managers who agreed to participate in the pilot test to carefully read and review the toolkit over a two-week period. We encouraged (but did not require) that they complete the toolkit's worksheets. We also asked the participants to provide feedback using a standardized feedback form (see Appendix B) as they reviewed the toolkit. The feedback form contained questions about the extent to which each chapter of the toolkit met its objectives (response options: strongly agree, agree, neither agree nor disagree, disagree, or strongly disagree), whether any sections of the toolkit were unclear or difficult to understand (yes/no), and whether program staff felt uncomfortable using any of the tools provided (yes/no). Participants returned completed feedback forms via email and were remunerated for their time spent reviewing the toolkit.

Note that we were unable to observe program staff interacting with the toolkit, which limited our ability to objectively assess comprehension and application of the material.

Toolkit Chapter One: Introduction and Overview

Pilot Participants' Feedback

All three of the pilot participants *strongly agreed* with the statement, "The chapter clearly explained the purpose and content in the toolkit"; one *strongly agreed* and two *agreed* that the chapter "helped me decide whether this toolkit is appropriate for use with my program." Participants uniformly rated the sections as being clear and felt comfortable using the tools contained in Chapter One.

One organization representative wrote,

> I think one thing that could be added would be a third challenge point: How do I know if my program is in fact CVE? For example, my program is not technically defined as a CVE program, but it could be considered that way. It would be cool for you guys to develop a more expansive definition of CVE so that some programs which never saw themselves as CVE-based might start to do so.

This representative expanded on this point in the space for general comments, suggesting that the toolkit could begin with "examples of different CVE programs because many programs are in fact CVE (or qualify as CVE) but they are not branded this way. Additionally, I recommend that you modify the term *CVE* to something broader, perhaps 'Countering Extremism.'"

Edits to the Toolkit

We revised the Preface (first paragraph) and Chapter One (the section "Intended Audience") to acknowledge variability in CVE programs and provide examples of different strategies organizations are using to prevent violent extremism. In addition, we carefully considered changes to the toolkit's title to address the reviewer's comments regarding the term *CVE*. However after some discussion with the study's sponsor, we decided to keep the term in the title.

Toolkit Chapter Two: Identify Your Program's Core Components for Evaluation and Build a Program Logic Model

Pilot Participants' Feedback

All three of the pilot participant organizations *strongly agreed* with the statement that "[T]he chapter helped me identify the core components of my program." However, while two organizations *strongly agreed* that "the chapter provided guidance on how to develop a logic model," one *disagreed*. That representative recommended "greater clarity" in structuring short- and long-term outcomes and suggested that "the Logic Model either needs to be in the beginning of the chapter or after the third chapter." The representative thought these changes would make the chapter's organization clearer; the other pilot participants through the sections were clear. All three of the representatives told us that they felt comfortable completing all the tools in Chapter Two.

With respect to our guidance for identifying a target population, one participant suggested that we specifically add a section on "race/ethnicity to encourage people to include individuals from various racial groups and to consider potential differences in outreach to participants and program implementation based on racial groups." Another suggested that we add a category (in addition to target audience age, gender, profession, region, and so on) on online/Internet populations. Another suggestion was that we "add some more details on how virtual programs are evaluated because the intended outcomes are often more difficult to ascertain, the audience more amorphous." Finally, with respect to program objectives, a representative wrote that programs typically try to reach multiple communities, adding that, for example, "You might have a set of desired outcomes for the Muslim community and a separate set for the non-Muslim community."

Edits to the Toolkit

In response to these suggestions, we retained the logic model where it was, since this placement aligns with RAND's Suicide Prevention Toolkit, as well as with the GTO approach. However, we did add a paragraph in the section "How to Assess Core Components" that instructs readers to think about activities and target audiences in a simple way and separately from each other. We also added "race, ethnicity, or country of origin" as a category to consider when thinking about a program's target population, and we expanded the category "region" to "region or online community" with the example "Facebook users who click on our organization's banner ad." We also incorporated additional guidance to help programs identify both short- and long-term outcomes.

Toolkit Chapter Three: Design an Evaluation for Your Program

Pilot Participants' Feedback

Two participant organizations *strongly agreed* and one *agreed* that "the chapter provided guidance about the type of evaluation appropriate for my program." One *strongly agreed*, one *agreed*, and one *neither agreed nor disagreed* with the statement, "The chapter helped me select an evaluation based on the resources and expertise my program has available." Two representatives told us that all sections in the chapter were clear, though one was "not sure what constitutes a 'similar composition to a participating group'" for evaluation designs that employ a control group: "I am not sure if examples could be utilized in my case, e.g., if my participants are secondary teachers, does my control group only have to be other secondary teachers or are there other factors I must consider?" All participants felt comfortable completing all the tools in Chapter Three, though with respect to Worksheet 3.1, a representative wrote, "I was unclear how Worksheet 3.1 is to be used. Is it more of something that I refer to just to get a sense of the different types of evaluations?"

However, as a general comment to Chapter Three, one representative told us that "most of the evaluation methods are impractical for use by community organizations," that "data security is not a realistic expectation," and that "evaluation expertise will not be available at these organizations." On the other hand, another representative said, "I appreciate this section as it enables the program specialist to determine whether they can achieve the evaluation with the tools you have provided or whether they need to hire an external advisor."

Edits to the Toolkit

In revising Chapter Three, we added a subsection titled "Selecting a Control or Comparison Group" in the section "Identify Issues Pertinent to Your Evaluation Design."

Toolkit Chapter Four: Select Evaluation Measures for Your Program

Pilot Participants' Feedback

All three participants *strongly agreed* that "the chapter helped me select process evaluation measures" and two *strongly agreed* and one *neither agreed nor disagreed* that "the chapter helped me select outcome evaluation measures." Two respondents told us that the sections in this chapter were clear; the third told us that the sample outcome evaluation measures we present may only be clear "for the objectives you selected," but then further stated, "I think the problem is with us. Our objective doesn't fit well. . . . I really think we have work to do."

All three indicated that they felt comfortable completing the tools in this chapter. One representative wrote, "This might be the most important chapter in the toolkit. Most program managers do not know the difference between process and outcome evaluation." This participant suggested that we emphasize that both process and outcome evaluations are essential.

Edits to the Toolkit

We did not make any edits to the chapter in response to this component of the toolkit pilot testing.

Toolkit Chapter Five: Use Evaluation Data to Improve Your Program

Pilot Participants' Feedback

To ensure that this summary of changes aligns with the current toolkit structure, we refer to this chapter as *Chapter Five* here. However, what is now Chapter Five in the toolkit was Chapter Six at the time of the pilot test. In response to feedback from the pilot test, we made the original Chapter Five an appendix, as discussed later.

One pilot participant *strongly agreed* and a second *agreed* that Chapter Five "described how to use my evaluation data for program improvement," while the third participant did not complete this chapter of the toolkit. Both participant who did complete the chapter indicated that all sections were clear and that they felt comfortable completing all the tools. One participant told us,

> This section is extremely essential to improve existing programs. Considering the lack of patience and inexperience of community program designers, they will likely not review this section. There needs to be a summary at the beginning of the toolkit which will increase the likelihood that reviewers will know what is in each chapter and will understand the benefit of reading and applying the entire toolkit.

The other participant agreed: "If I hire a stats expert, I wonder if this part of the toolkit is even still relevant for me." Another question that came up in this chapter was, "How do programs that have evaluation templates from a grantor that they have to abide by use this toolkit?"

Edits to the Toolkit

We added a note to the beginning of this chapter stating that the content is still likely to benefit programs that are preparing to start their evaluation.

Toolkit Appendix A: Creating Your Own Survey

Pilot Participants' Feedback

Two organizations *strongly agreed* and one *agreed* that Appendix A "taught me how to develop my own survey instrument." All three indicated that all sections in Appendix A were clear.

Edits to the Toolkit

We decided to improve the original version of this appendix by adding worksheets to assist users in developing new surveys.

Toolkit Appendix B: Social Media Metrics

Pilot Participants' Feedback

With respect to Appendix B, one organization *strongly agreed*, one *agreed*, and one *neither agreed nor disagreed* with the statement, "The chapter provided me an overview of key metrics for different social media platforms." While all three indicated that the appendix was clear, two did provide additional comments. One said, "It might be helpful to provide reference to other social media application/metrics toolkits and resources which are regularly updated online. Since this area is ever evolving, this section will be the first to be obsolete." The other stated, "I felt this section did not do a good enough job on connecting evaluation of social media performance to actual CVE (prevention and deradicalization etc.). I am wondering if this might require a completely separate toolkit entirely because some programs are almost completely online."

Edits to the Toolkit

At the beginning of this appendix, we provided additional resources that users may consult for information about social media metrics.

Toolkit Appendix C: Analyze Your Program's Evaluation Data

Appendix C was Chapter Five of the toolkit at the time of pilot testing. Based on participant feedback and due to its technical nature, we opted to move this content to the appendix matter.

Pilot Participants' Feedback

Two pilot participants *strongly agreed* and one *agreed* that this section "described how to enter evaluation data into a database" and "described how to analyze evaluation data." However, not all participants found the instructions were clear, nor did they feel comfortable completing all the tools. General reactions varied:

> [Organization A:] It is unlikely that the community organizations will be able to apply any of these evaluation tools. Also, if anyone does not have the understanding of statistical analysis, this chapter is certainly insufficient and unhelpful. Existing technical expertise is required to utilize the contents of this chapter.

> [Organization B:] This was very well done. I have some reservations about my capacity in this area but after reading this chapter I feel like I can take on Excel. I hope so! I did not use the tools with data but I felt that I might be able to with more study on my part.

> [Organization C:] I definitely felt that I would have to hire a stats expert after reading Primers 1, 2 and 3. However, I will say the screenshots and descriptions are all very clear. Is it possible to include the email address of a RAND troubleshooter to [contact] if someone has questions?

Edits to the Toolkit

Because of the technical nature of the chapter's content, we opted to make this chapter an appendix because the tools require programs to have collected their evaluation data, and because the content requires basic proficiency in Microsoft Excel. Therefore, the content of Appendix C may not be relevant to all programs that use the toolkit.

General Comments on Toolkit

Pilot Participants' Feedback

Finally, pilot participants were given the option to provide additional, overarching comments. Two expressed general skepticism about the use of the toolkit. In one case, a participant told us, "This toolkit is unlikely to be used by most community-based CVE programs (unless I am misunderstanding). The toolkit is itself useful but the programs (with a few exceptions) are unlikely to be of scale to apply the evaluation. Third-party evaluations will need to be implemented." Another participant asked, "I also wonder if one is not able to conduct some of the evaluations in-house, how might they still be encouraged to use parts of this toolkit?"

This skepticism was balanced by praise for the toolkit, however. One representative wrote,

> I do not have additional comments to improve. I did my evaluation over several days and each day when I returned to the tasks I felt each chapter was self-contained and digestible so I could remember what came before (or review it easily if I needed to) and move on. This is one of the best "how to's" I have seen. Thank you!

Another said, "This is a very helpful toolkit for program directors and managers. I would definitely use it as we often don't have the budget to hire and evaluator."

Edits to the Toolkit

We did not make any edits in response to this component of the toolkit pilot testing.

CHAPTER FOUR

Conclusion

The RAND Program Evaluation Toolkit for Countering Violent Extremism was designed to build the knowledge and skills of individuals who are responsible for implementing CVE programs and to facilitate the self-evaluation of these programs. Such evaluations are critical for assessing program impact and can inform decisions about whether to sustain or scale up current efforts.

The toolkit aims to help CVE programs develop a complete and detailed logic model that summarizes program characteristics and activities, target available resources, identify important needs in their communities, and collect and apply evaluation data to improve program implementation and effectiveness. It guides users through a series of sequential steps in designing and implementing a program evaluation. Repeating the process on a regular basis will help program staff continually assess and improve their CVE program and will increase the likelihood that the program will achieve its intended outcomes.

We developed the toolkit with the hope that it would serve as a helpful resource to guide CVE programs in assessing their activities, identifying areas for improvement, measuring the outcomes, and making adjustments to their programs—all of which can ultimately reduce the risk of violent extremism in their communities.

Summary of CVE Evaluation Studies

Table A.1 summarizes the the methodology and findings of the eight studies discussed in Chapter Two, along with overarching observations.

Table A.1
Summary of Evaluation Studies

Citation	Location	Participants	Intervention	Control Group	Testing Methodology	Significant Findings
Aldrich, 2014	Mali (Timbuktu and Dire)	Residents of Timbuktu	USAID programming	Used survey to compare Timbuktu with Dire, a city that did not receive USAID programming	Postintervention survey of 200 residents of Timbuktu and Dire	Residents in Timbuktu were more likely than control group to listen to peaceful radio programs and participate in decisionmaking. No effect on perceptions of whether the United States was fighting Islam or whether al-Qa'ida activities were justified.
Frenett and Dow, 2014[a]	North America and United Kingdom	Individuals whose Facebook activity suggests that they support white supremacist or Islamist extremist causes	Former extremists sent direct antiextremist messages to participants on Facebook	No comparison	Examined participant responses (read rate, response rate, type of response) to antiradicalization messages, as well as relationship between outreach approach and response	• More than 60 percent of messages read. • 59% responded directly or shifted behavior, such as changing privacy settings. • Of those who did respond, 60% sustained engagement. • Casual, sentimental, and reflective tones performed best (vs. antagonistic or meditative). • Offer of assistance and personal stories were the best content (versus highlighting the consequences of a negative reaction or personal question).
Feddes, Mann, and Doosje, 2015	The Netherlands	46 Muslim youth with migrant backgrounds	Three workshops to increase participants' self-esteem, agency, perspective-taking skills, and empathy[b]	Pre/post design	Questionnaires administered before, during, and after treatment exposure	Participants experienced significant increase in agency and improvement in attitude toward ideology-based violence and own violent intentions. Marginal improvements in self-esteem, empathy, and perspective taking. No effect for individual and collective relative deprivation and social disc.
Amjad and Wood, 2009	Pakistan	University of Pakistan students	Lecture designed to improve perceptions of Jews	Randomly assigned participants to active treatment or control condition (exposure to educational lecture)	Tested whether participants accepted request by confederate to join militant group	Treatment reduced the number who joined a militant group versus control.

Table A.1—Continued

Citation	Location	Participants	Intervention	Control Group	Testing Methodology	Significant Findings
Liht and Savage, 2013	United Kingdom	81 young UK Muslims	Combined a multimedia course with group activities and discussion over a 16-hour period spanning 5–15 weeks.	Pre/post design	Qualitatively coded dialogue from small groups that were charged with debating moral dilemmas relevant to Muslims living in the UK	Intervention was linked to an increase in individual ability to problem solve and resolve conflict through "collaboration and compromise."
USAID, 2011a	Africa	Survey participants in Niger, Chad, and Mali	Youth employment/ outreach programs, vocational skills training, and community development and media activities	Surveys in four comparison areas where minimum of Trans-Sahara Counterterrorism Partnership activity (no further information)	Opinion poll survey across the three treatment and four comparison areas	Treatment areas scored 5.67% higher on key survey items than comparison areas. Most robust improvements for outcome variable "Listen to peace and tolerance radio." Least improvement noted for questions addressing opposition against violence/al-Qa'ida.
USAID, 2013[a]	Africa	1,500 ethnic Somali youth in Somalia and Kenya who were full, partial, and nonbeneficiaries of USAID programming	Somali Youth Livelihoods Program was a job training program, Garissa Youth Program provided livelihood/ skills training, and Kenya Transition Initiative–Eastleigh provided grants to support youth and community capacity building to foster moderation and nonviolence	Surveyed participants who were partial beneficiaries and nonbeneficiaries of programming	Opinion poll survey across three groups	Compared with youth with no access to programming, program beneficiaries reported higher levels of civic engagement and, to lesser extent, efficacy, connections to youth associations, and identity. No differences for rejection of violence in the name of Islam.
Williams, Horgan, and Evans, 2016[a]	United States	179 youth and adults who had participated in any one of three CVE programs in Montgomery County, Maryland	Combination of community education, volunteer and multicultural programs, and collaboration building between law enforcement and community partners	No control group	WORDE participants completed a 14-item Brief Volunteer Program Outcome Assessment scale (1–7 rating) tailored to CVE-relevant volunteer programs	On 12 of 14 items, participants' mean responses were reliably above the midpoint of scale items.

[a] Not a peer-reviewed publication.

[b] *Perspective taking* refers to the act of viewing an issue or situation from an alternative perspective.

Feedback Form Used in the Pilot Test of the RAND Evaluation Toolkit for CVE Programs

Instructions

We have created a feedback form for each chapter of the toolkit. As you finish reading each chapter and working through the tools in each chapter, please pause to answer the corresponding pilot-test questions for that chapter. We are looking for your honest opinions, so please answer all the questions.

How do I know if I'm done with the pilot test?

Before sending your feedback to us, please review your work.

Which chapters of the toolkit did you use?

☐ Chapter One. Introduction and Overview
☐ Chapter Two. Identify Your Program's Core Components for Evaluation and Build a Program Logic Model
☐ Chapter Three. Design an Evaluation for Your Program
☐ Chapter Four. Select Evaluation Measures for Your Program
☐ Chapter Five. Analyze Your Program's Evaluation Data*
☐ Chapter Six. Use Evaluation Data to Improve Your Program*
☐ Appendix A. Creating Your Own Survey
☐ Appendix B. Social Media Metrics

After the pilot test, the "Analyze Your Program's Evaluation Data" chapter became Appendix C of the toolkit, and the "Use Evaluation Data to Improve Your Program" chapter became Chapter Five.

Do you have completed feedback forms for each chapter you selected above?

☐ Yes. Great job! You are finished.
☐ No. We really want your feedback. Please complete the feedback forms for all chapters of the toolkit that you used during the pilot test.

What if I do not work through all the chapters?

Depending on your program's interest, you may only use a portion of the toolkit. We would appreciate your feedback on any portions of the toolkit you are able to review.

What should I do with my pilot-test feedback form?

Please email your feedback to Todd Helmus at Todd_Helmus@rand.org. He will send an email confirmation letting you know that your feedback has been received. If you prefer to send your feedback by fax, please contact him at 703-413-1100, ext. 5231, to arrange a time for faxing.

What if I have other questions during the pilot test?

Feel free to contact Todd Helmus with any questions you might have at 703-413-1100, ext. 5231, or at Todd_Helmus@rand.org.

Thank you for your feedback!

Chapter One. Introduction and Overview

1.   Please indicate the **extent** to which this chapter met its **objectives**.

	Strongly Agree	Agree	Neither Agree nor Disagree	Disagree	Strongly Disagree
The chapter clearly explained the purpose and content in the toolkit.	☐	☐	☐	☐	☐
The chapter helped me decide whether this toolkit is appropriate for use with my program.	☐	☐	☐	☐	☐

2.   Were there any **sections of the chapter** that were **not clear or difficult to understand**?

☐ No, all sections were clear.
☐ Yes. Which section(s)? Please list page numbers. _____

⟶ How can we **improve** these sections? (Feel free to write directly on the toolkit.)

_____

_____

_____

_____

3.   Did you feel **uncomfortable** using any of the following tools?

☐ No, I felt comfortable completing all the tools in this chapter.
☐ Yes, I had difficulty with the following tools:

   ☐ Checklist 1.1. Is This Toolkit Right for My Program?
   ☐ Other (please specify): _____

   _____

4.   Do you have any **additional comments** about how to improve this chapter of the toolkit?

_____

_____

_____

_____

Chapter Two. Identify Your Program's Core Components for Evaluation and Build a Program Logic Model

1. Please indicate the **extent** to which this chapter met its **objectives**.

	Strongly Agree	Agree	Neither Agree nor Disagree	Disagree	Strongly Disagree
The chapter helped me identify the core components of my program.	☐	☐	☐	☐	☐
The chapter provided guidance on how to develop a logic model.	☐	☐	☐	☐	☐

2. Were there any **sections of the chapter** that were **not clear or difficult to understand**?

☐ No, all sections were clear.
☐ Yes. Which section(s)? Please list page numbers. _____

⟶ How can we **improve** these sections? (Feel free to write directly on the toolkit.)

_____
_____
_____
_____

3. Did you feel **uncomfortable** using any of the following tools?

☐ No, I felt comfortable completing all the tools in this chapter.
☐ Yes, I had difficulty with the following tools:

  ☐ Checklist 2.1. Is Your Logic Model Complete and Appropriately Detailed?
  ☐ Checklist 2.2. Are the Core Components of Your Logic Model Appropriately Aligned?
  ☐ Worksheet 2.1. Identifying Components
  ☐ Templates 2.1 and 2.2. Program Logic Model
  ☐ Other (please specify): _____

  _____

4. Do you have any **additional comments** about how to improve this chapter of the toolkit?

_____
_____
_____
_____

Chapter Three. Design an Evaluation for Your Program

1. Please indicate the **extent** to which this chapter met its **objectives**.

	Strongly Agree	Agree	Neither Agree nor Disagree	Disagree	Strongly Disagree
The chapter provided guidance about the type of evaluation appropriate for my program.	☐	☐	☐	☐	☐
The chapter helped me select an evaluation based on the resources and expertise my program has available.	☐	☐	☐	☐	☐

2. Were there any **sections of the chapter** that were **not clear or difficult to understand**?

☐ No, all sections were clear.
☐ Yes. Which section(s)? Please list page numbers. _____

⟶ How can we **improve** these sections? (Feel free to write directly on the toolkit.)

_____

_____

_____

_____

3. Did you feel **uncomfortable** using any of the following tools?

☐ No, I felt comfortable completing all the tools in this chapter.
☐ Yes, I had difficulty with the following tools:

☐ Table 3.1. Types of Evaluation Designs
☐ Worksheet 3.1. Issues to Consider for My Program
☐ Template 3.1. Evaluation Planner
☐ Other (please specify): _____

_____

4. Do you have any **additional comments** about how to improve this chapter of the toolkit?

_____

_____

_____

_____

Chapter Four. Select Evaluation Measures for Your Program

1.   Please indicate the **extent** to which this chapter met its **objectives**.

	Strongly Agree	Agree	Neither Agree nor Disagree	Disagree	Strongly Disagree
The chapter helped me select **process** evaluation measures.	☐	☐	☐	☐	☐
The chapter helped me select **outcome** evaluation measures.	☐	☐	☐	☐	☐

2.   Were there any **sections of the chapter** that were **not clear or difficult to understand**?

☐ No, all sections were clear.
☐ Yes. Which section(s)? Please list page numbers. _____

⟶ How can we **improve** these sections? (Feel free to write directly on the toolkit.)

_____

_____

_____

_____

3.   Did you feel **uncomfortable** using any of the following tools?

☐ No, I felt comfortable completing all the tools in this chapter.
☐ Yes, I had difficulty with the following tools:

   ☐ Table 4.1. Sample Process Measures
   ☐ Table 4.2. Sample Outcome Measures for CVE Programs Addressing Individuals at
      Risk for Violent Extremism
   ☐ Table 4.3. Sample Outcome Measures for CVE Programs Addressing Communities
      That Influence Individuals at Risk for Violent Extremism
   ☐ Checklist 4.1. To What Extent Do the Measures Selected Align with Your Program's
      Target Population, Activities, and Outcomes?
   ☐ Other (please specify): _____

   _____

4.   Do you have any **additional comments** about how to improve this chapter of the toolkit?

_____

_____

_____

_____

Chapter Five. Analyze Your Program's Evaluation Data

Note: This chapter's content can now be found in Appendix C of the toolkit.

1. Please indicate the **extent** to which this chapter met its **objectives**.

	Strongly Agree	Agree	Neither Agree nor Disagree	Disagree	Strongly Disagree
The chapter described how to enter evaluation data into a database.	☐	☐	☐	☐	☐
The chapter described how to analyze evaluation data.	☐	☐	☐	☐	☐

2. Were there any **sections of the chapter** that were **not clear or difficult to understand**?

☐ No, all sections were clear.
☐ Yes. Which section(s)? Please list page numbers. _____

➡ How can we **improve** these sections? (Feel free to write directly on the toolkit.)

_____

_____

_____

_____

3. Did you feel **uncomfortable** using any of the following tools?

☐ No, I felt comfortable completing all the tools in this chapter.
☐ Yes, I had difficulty with the following tools:

   ☐ Primer 1: Calculating Descriptive Statistics for Your Program
   ☐ Primer 2: Statistical Models for Detecting Differences in Your Program's Target Population
   ☐ Primer 3: Linking Process to Outcome Measures
   ☐ Other (please specify): _____

   _____

4. Do you have any **additional comments** about how to improve this chapter of the toolkit?

_____

_____

_____

_____

Chapter Six. Use Evaluation Data to Improve Your Program

Note: This chapter's content can now be found in Chapter Five of the toolkit, with tool numbers reassigned accordingly.

1. Please indicate the **extent** to which this chapter met its **objectives**.

	Strongly Agree	Agree	Neither Agree nor Disagree	Disagree	Strongly Disagree
The chapter described how to use my evaluation data for program improvement.	☐	☐	☐	☐	☐

2. Were there any **sections of the chapter** that were **not clear or difficult to understand**?

☐ No, all sections were clear.
☐ Yes. Which section(s)? Please list page numbers. _____

⟶ How can we **improve** these sections? (Feel free to write directly on the toolkit.)

_____

_____

_____

_____

3. Did you feel **uncomfortable** using any of the following tools?

☐ No, I felt comfortable completing all the tools in this chapter.
☐ Yes, I had difficulty with the following tools:

   ☐ Checklist 6.1. What CQI Actions Are Needed to Improve the Program?
   ☐ Worksheet 6.1. Assessing Participation in Your Program's Evaluation
   ☐ Worksheet 6.2. Review Program Outcomes, with Examples
   ☐ Worksheet 6.3. Review Program Outcomes
   ☐ Worksheet 6.4. Program Improvement Plan
   ☐ Table 6.1. Results-Based Scenarios and Associated Strategies for Program Improvement
   ☐ Other (please specify): _____

   _____

4. Do you have any **additional comments** about how to improve this chapter of the toolkit?

_____

_____

_____

_____

Appendix A. Creating Your Own Survey

1. Please indicate the **extent** to which this appendix met its **objectives**.

	Strongly Agree	Agree	Neither Agree nor Disagree	Disagree	Strongly Disagree
The appendix taught me how to develop my own survey instrument.	☐	☐	☐	☐	☐

2. Were there any **sections of the appendix** that were **not clear or difficult to understand**?

☐ No, all sections were clear.
☐ Yes. Which section(s)? Please list page numbers. _____

⟶ How can we **improve** these sections? (Feel free to write directly on the toolkit.)

_____

_____

_____

_____

3. Do you have any **additional comments** about how to improve this appendix?

_____

_____

_____

_____

Appendix B. Social Media Metrics

1. Please indicate the **extent** to which this appendix met its **objectives**.

	Strongly Agree	Agree	Neither Agree nor Disagree	Disagree	Strongly Disagree
The appendix provided me with an overview of key metrics for different social media platforms.	☐	☐	☐	☐	☐

2. Were there any **sections of the appendix** that were **not clear or difficult to understand**?

☐ No, all sections were clear.
☐ Yes. Which section(s)? Please list page numbers. _____

⟶ How can we **improve** these sections? (Feel free to write directly on the toolkit.)

_____

_____

_____

_____

3. Do you have any **additional comments** about how to improve this appendix?

_____

_____

_____

_____

Additional Feedback About the Toolkit

Do you have any **additional comments** about how to improve the toolkit?

_____

_____

_____

_____

_____

_____

_____

_____

_____

_____

_____

_____

_____

_____

_____

_____

_____

_____

_____

_____

_____

_____

References

Acosta, Joie, Rajeev Ramchand, Amariah Becker, Alexandria Felton, and Aaron Kofner, *RAND Suicide Prevention Program Evaluation Toolkit*, Santa Monica, Calif.: RAND Corporation, TL-111-OSD, 2013. As of January 17, 2017:
http://www.rand.org/pubs/tools/TL111.html

Aldrich, Daniel P., "First Steps Towards Hearts and Minds? USAID's Countering Violent Extremism Policies in Africa," *Terrorism and Political Violence*, Vol. 26, No. 3, 2014, pp. 523–546.

Al-Rawi, Ahmed K., "The Anti-Terrorist Advertising Campaigns in the Middle East," *Journal of International Communication*, Vol. 19, No. 2, 2013, pp. 182–195.

Amjad, Naumana, and Alex M. Wood, "Identifying and Changing the Normative Beliefs About Aggression Which Lead Young Muslim Adults to Join Extremist Anti-Semitic Groups in Pakistan," *Aggressive Behavior*, Vol. 35, No. 6, November–December 2009, pp. 514–519.

Bjelopera, Jerome P., *The Domestic Terrorist Threat: Background and Issues for Congress*, Washington, D.C.: Congressional Research Service, January 17, 2013.

Executive Office of the President, *Strategic Implementation Plan for Empowering Local Partners to Prevent Violent Extremism in the United States*, Washington, D.C.: White House, October 2016.

Feddes, Allard R., and Marcello Gallucci, "A Literature Review on Methodology Used in Evaluating Effects of Preventive and De-Radicalisation Interventions," *Journal for Deradicalization*, No. 5, Winter 2015–2016.

Feddes, Allard R., Liesbeth Mann, and Bertjan Doosje, "Increasing Self-Esteem and Empathy to Prevent Violent Radicalization: A Longitudinal Quantitative Evaluation of a Resilience Training Focused on Adolescents with a Dual Identity," *Journal of Applied Social Psychology*, Vol. 45, No. 7, July 2015, pp. 400–411.

Fink, Naureen Chowdhury, Peter Romaniuk, and Rafia Barakat, *Evaluating Countering Violent Extremism Programming: Practice and Progress*, Goshen, Ind.: Center on Global Counterterrorism Cooperation, 2013. As of January 17, 2017:
http://www.globalcenter.org/publications/evaluating-countering-violent-extremism-engagement-practices-and-progress

Frenett, Ross, and Moli Dow, *One to One Interventions: A Pilot CVE Methodology*, London: Institute for Strategic Dialogue and Curtain University, 2014. As of January 17, 2017:
http://www.strategicdialogue.org/wp-content/uploads/2016/04/One2One_Web_v9.pdf

Glaser, Barney G., and Anselm L. Strauss, *The Discovery of Grounded Theory: Strategies for Qualitative Research*, Piscataway, N.J.: AldineTransaction, 1967.

Helmus, Todd C., Miriam Matthews, Rajeev Ramchand, Sina Beaghley, David Stebbins, Amanda Kadlec, Michael A. Brown, Aaron Kofner, and Joie Acosta, *RAND Program Evaluation Toolkit for Countering Violent Extremism*, Santa Monica, Calif.: RAND Corporation, TL-243-DHS, 2017. As of February 2017:
http://www.rand.org/pubs/tools/TL243.html

Kirk, Ashley, "Iraq and Syria: How Many Foreign Fighters Are Fighting for ISIL?" *Telegraph*, March 24, 2016. As of January 17, 2017:
http://www.telegraph.co.uk/news/2016/03/29/iraq-and-syria-how-many-foreign-fighters-are-fighting-for-isil

Liht, Jose, and Sara Savage, "Preventing Violent Extremism Through Value Complexity: Being Muslim Being British," *Journal of Strategic Security*, Vol. 6, No. 4, Winter 2013, pp. 44–66.

Mastroe, Caitlin, and Susa Szmania, *Surveying CVE Metrics in Prevention, Disengagement and DeRadicalization Programs*, College Park, Md.: National Consortium for the Study of Terrorism and Responses to Terrorism, 2016. As of January 17, 2017:
http://www.start.umd.edu/publication/surveying-cve-metrics-prevention-disengagement-and-de-radicalization-programs

New America Foundation, *Homegrown Extremism, 2001–2015*, Washington, D.C., 2015.

Reynolds, Louis, and Henry Tuck, *The Counter-Narrative Monitoring and Evaluation Handbook*, London, Institute for Strategic Dialogue, 2016. As of January 17, 2017:
http://www.strategicdialogue.org/wp-content/uploads/2016/12/CN-Monitoring-and-Evaluation-Handbook.pdf

Richardson, Roslyn, *Fighting Fire with Fire: Target Audience Responses to Online Anti-Violence Campaigns*, Barton, Australia: Australian Strategic Policy Institute, December 2013. As of January 17, 2017:
https://www.aspi.org.au/publications/fighting-fire-with-fire-target-audience-responses-to-online-anti-violence-campaigns/Fight_fire_long_paper_web.pdf

Romaniuk, Peter, *Does CVE Work? Lessons Learned from the Global Effort to Counter Violent Extremism*, Goshen, Ind.: Global Center on Cooperative Security, 2015. As of January 17, 2017:
http://www.globalcenter.org/publications/does-cve-work-lessons-learned-from-the-global-effort-to-counter-violent-extremism/

U.S. Agency for International Development, *Mid-Term Evaluation of USAID's Counter-Extremism Programming in Africa*, Washington, D.C., February 1, 2011. As of January 17, 2017:
http://pdf.usaid.gov/pdf_docs/Pdacr583.pdf

———, *Mid-Term Evaluation of Three Countering Violent Extremism Projects, Counter-Extremism Programming in Africa*, Washington, D.C., February 22, 2013. As of January 17, 2017:
http://pdf.usaid.gov/pdf_docs/pdacx479.pdf

U.S. Code, Title 18, Crimes and Criminal Procedures, Chapter 113B, Terrorism, Section 2331, Definitions, February 1, 2010.

Williams, Michael J., John G. Horgan, and William P. Evans, *Evaluation of a Multi-Faceted, U.S. Community-Based, Muslim-Led CVE Program*, report submitted to U.S. Department of Justice, June 2016.